The Sins of the

Father

JOHN WESLEY KNIGHT

Copyright © 2010 by John Wesley Knight

The Sins of the Father

ISBN number: 978-1-59712-419-5

Printed in the United States of America by
Catawba Publishing Company

Order from:
Catawba Publishing Company
(704) 717-8452
www.catawbapublishing.com

In Loving Memory of My Godfather

Michael Kufta

"A man after God's heart"

Seth + Angela

I pray That you will Enjoy
THE Book

THANK you Both For your Friendship
And For Being Family

"Love you Both"
John

ACKNOWLEDGMENTS

To my Lord and Savior, Jesus Christ; thank you for your unconditional love that never ceases. You are the lover of my soul.

To my beloved wife Tonya and our four children Trinite, Natae, Alex and Jayda; thank you for all of your prayers and support - your love inspires me.

Thank you to all who inspired me and encouraged me on this project ~ my mother Gladys Knight, Mike & Jeanetta Kufta, Charles Summers, Rick Frazier, Mark Gilewicz, Marvin Mumford, James Knight, Steve Neal, Don Lane, Bishop Larry Jackson, Pastor Kelvin Smith, Pastor Herb Harris, Pastor James Davis, Pastor Dennis Hall, and a special thank you to my friend and editor, Paulette Wallace, for your dedication and excellence.

I could not have completed this project without you all. May God's favor rest upon you.

TABLE OF CONTENTS

PRELUDE

I have pondered many questions throughout my life that I would like you to think upon.

Have you ever thought about what kind of world this would be if everyone were just like you? Do you believe that you have become the person you were created to be? Have you ever thought about what would happen to you if you were removed from everything that is familiar to you? When things keep happening over and over again in your life, do you think it is a happenstance or do you think God is trying to speak to you?

I find it interesting that we have such limited views of ourselves. We do not have the ability to see ourselves from the outside in, we only see ourselves from the inside out. We are a biased people trapped inside our own selves. What disturbs me most is that people tend to see the faults of others before they are able to see the faults of themselves. They end up in a vicious cycle because they are never able to see beyond their own paradigm.

Throughout my life I have heard many metaphors. One in particular that comes to mind is, "The apple doesn't fall far from the tree." This has been understood to mean that more times than not, children will turn out to be just like their parents. What I hope to accomplish in this book is to shed light on the Sins of the Father and show how our lives are impacted by our parents. My goal is to try to enlighten, encourage, and inspire you to become the person God intended.

I remember saying to myself as a young man that I would never turn out to be like my father. I am thankful to God to this very day that because of my Lord and Savior, I did not turn out like him nor did I follow in his footsteps.

Unfortunately like many fathers, my father was lost and needed guidance. What was intriguing to me was that although he was lost, he had children who looked to him for direction. Given these circumstances, it appeared to me that my life was pretty much over before it really began. I feared that I would be doomed to emulate what I was born into. Some might have said that all hope was lost, because whatever children are born into becomes what is normal to them. In other words, children will usually imitate their parents' behavior and comprehend it later. The problem with later is that by the time you become an adult and comprehend the behavior of your parents as being wrong, you have already become them.

Our initial relationship with our parents has the ability to shape our choices, habits, environments, opinions, morals, relationships, and how we view and receive love. One of the most important choices of our lives that will impact us for the rest of our lives, yet we have no choice in selecting, comes with a bit of irony - none of us get to choose our parents.

PART ONE

Parents

God in his infinite wisdom established an order in his creation. God did not create Cain and Able and then Adam and Eve, Adam and Eve came first because God is a God of order. The book of Genesis 1:27-28 tells us, "So God created man in his *own* image, in the image of God created he him; male and female created he them. 28 And God blessed them, and God said unto them, Be fruitful, and multiply, and replenish the earth, and subdue it: and have dominion over the fish of the sea, and over the fowl of the air, and over every living thing that moveth upon the earth." What God wanted was for Adam and Eve to be fruitful and multiply and replenish the earth. The book of Genesis 1:11-12 also tells us, "Let the earth bring forth grass, the herb yielding seed, *and* the fruit tree yielding fruit after his kind, whose seed *is* in itself, upon the earth: and it was so. 12 And the earth brought forth grass, and herb yielding seed after his kind, and the tree yielding fruit, whose seed was in and of itself, after his kind, and God saw that it was good." Here God is telling us that just as the herb yielding seed brings forth grass after its kind, and the fruit tree yields fruit after its kind, human beings yield seeds after their own kind which are known as children. What is unfortunate is that children are born in a vulnerable state.

It would be wonderful to hear a child coming out of his or her mother's womb screaming *"Hallelujah! Thank you Jesus!"* However, before they even realize that they need Jesus, children will initially have to deal with their parents. We all know that parents are not perfect. They are people who are flawed as we all are. The child who is looking to the parent for unconditional love may not always receive it, but you can rest assured that they will receive their parents' opinions, morals, prejudices, religious influences or lack thereof, and whatever pain that was inflicted upon *them* as children.

Parents play such a vital role in their children's lives. They shape many of the choices their children will make without even realizing it. Many have said it is unbelievable that one has to pass a test in order to drive an automobile, yet there is no test needed to become a parent. Having the ability to properly oversee a little soul is probably the most important job one could ever have.

Ultimately what I would like to submit is that parents are the first teachers of their children. They should look at the home as a boot camp or a training camp. The parent will lay the foundation of a child's life through precept and practice. Any other support system is supplementary to the home. This is why it is unthinkable for a parent to believe that raising children can be done without instruction and direction from God. Proverbs 22:6 says, "Train up a child in the way he should go: and when he is old, he will not depart from it. It is the parent's duty to allow God's instruction when raising children." My prayer for any parent is that they introduce their children to the most important person they will ever meet, that person being Jesus Christ.

What kind of parent do you see in yourself? Have you ever looked in the mirror and asked yourself that question? Are you the parent who says, "I am doing the best I can", as a way of justifying not having to improve your parenting skills at all? If so, you would be saying that your children will have to take it or leave it. I know that is not the message you want to send to your children because you love your children and you only want what is best for them. Remember, you play a major role in the success or failure of your children's lives. Realize that your children will leave home one way or the other - one way is broken, the other is whole.

Being Broken

As a Pastor I have counseled many people. What I have found to be true concerning those who were broken is that they did not realize they were broken. They had lived in a broken state for so many years that it was normalized and accepted as a way of life. They also, without realizing it, gravitated towards anyone who resembled them.

I had a friend who was extremely confrontational. No matter what you would tell him, he would disagree. Even if you were telling him something that would benefit *him*, he would disagree. I asked my friend if he knew what it meant to be broken, or even further what it meant to be *insane*. He said he did not. As I began to give him the definition of insanity, *which is 'continuing to do the same thing over and over again but expecting a different result'*, and explained to him that his personality and behaviors fit the definition. I guess you can imagine what his response was. You are correct, he completely disagreed with me. Why? Because people like my friend will always reject what is rational. It's interesting to me how insane people will constantly try to find other insane people to validate them as *not* being insane. Now how insane is that? When they find each other it's like the blind leading the blind – eventually they both fall into a ditch.

When you hear someone refer to a person as being broken, what does it really mean? Well, when a person is broken they have been shattered or fractured somewhere along the line. As a result, they are incomplete. I remember the old children's rhyme, *sticks and stones may break my bones, but names will never hurt me.* That all sounds great but the truth is, although sticks and stones can break bones, names can cause much more damage. When a person is broken the cause can vary from verbal abuse to sexual, mental, physical or emotional abuse. When you are dealing with a broken person there are signs. They may either be withdrawn, living in the past, or even concealing their inflictions. They will oftentimes talk about their past pain from twenty years ago as if it just happened twenty minutes ago. With broken individuals you have to choose your words carefully. They are so fragile they become upset very easily if the wrong word is said. They may also feel as if the entire world is against them and that no one understands or has experienced the pain they are feeling.   As a result you feel as though you have to walk on eggshells every time you are in their presence. When someone is broken they are usually very needy. No kind gesture or kind word is enough. For example, let's say that a cracked glass represents a broken person and water represents love. You can pour water into the glass, but the glass will never be able to contain the water. You will try to stop the water from sprouting but no matter where you place your hands you will never be able to do so. In other words, no matter how much love you give to a broken person, he or she will never be fulfilled. I have also found that when someone is broken, it can be the result of having been lied to at some point in their life. What happens is that they believe a lie as truth and ultimately believe the truth as a lie. Let me paint a clearer picture for you.

A little boy and little girl see their father physically abuse their mother. Although they may feel this is wrong, their little brains soak up this image like a sponge and the image is then imprinted in their brains. The children never see the mother leave the father, and the behavior of the father is never explained as being wrong. So at that very moment their minds become twisted in believing a lie as truth. The lie is that it is acceptable for a husband to physically abuse his wife. This young girl may grow up believing that if her husband physically abuses her, this is a display of his love and affection and it is OK. And if a man treats her well, without physical abuse, she would view him as weak or as someone who does not love her. All of this is resulting from her childhood, when she witnessed a lie and perceived it as truth. The same thing would hold true for the young boy who grows up to believe that he can be physically abusive towards his wife and she is to accept his behavior. The conversation would probably go something like this. "Honey, why are you leaving me, I thought you loved me." The wife would say, "I do love you, but I refuse to stay here another day with you beating on me." The husband would then reply, "My father beat my mother and she never left him." The wife would then respond, "And that is why you have a problem."

Both the little boy and the little girl who grew up in this abusive environment become emotionally paralyzed adults. They will both associate abuse with love and until they are given truth, they will go on and raise their children in the same manner, creating a perpetual cycle. The good news though is there is hope! If you are broken you do not have to continue living your life as a broken person or in a broken state. Psalms 147:3 says, "He healeth the broken in heart, and bindeth up their wounds." We all experience pain in our lives, but know that Christ died so that we might have life and life more abundantly. God wants us to know that he loves us with an everlasting love. You may not realize this, but most of us are looking for someone who is going to love us unconditionally, accept us for whom we are, and truly value us. The only person who can provide a love of this magnitude is our Lord and Savior, Jesus Christ. When you truly come to know him, you will experience an unspeakable joy that no man can give you or no man can take away from you. You will have a merry heart that doeth good like medicine. This is why finding Jesus early on in life is so important; so that we can learn of his truth before we are saturated with lies. Jesus said, they who are whole have no need of a physician, but they who are sick; Jesus has come to make you whole (Matthew 9:12).

Becoming Whole

How does one become whole? This question sounds more complex than it actually is. The answer is *by lacking nothing*. You might ask yourself, how does one come to a place where they lack nothing? Wholeness comes as a result of accepting Christ Jesus as your Lord and Savior. Totally laying down your life as you know it and following Christ. This process begins as we come to an understanding that we are sinners in need of a Savior. Some have said you can become whole once you find your soul mate.   How do I say, 'NOT!' so loud that you can hear my voice screaming from the pages? Some have said all you have to do is purge all of your bad thoughts and this will then leave you with only good thoughts and ultimately make you whole. Can you say, hmmm… with me? This sounds interesting but it is still not the answer. I realize that no one wants to walk around broken when they can be made whole, but only

Christ Jesus makes us whole. "For ye are dead, and your life is hid with Christ in God" (Colossians 3:3). If our lives are hid with Christ in God, how can we become whole without him? The answer to this question is… we cannot! Matthew 9:20-22 states, "And behold a woman, which was diseased with an issue of blood twelve years, came behind *him*, and touched the hem of his garment: 21 For she said within herself, If I may but touch his garment, I shall be whole. 22 But Jesus turned him about, and when he saw her, he said, Daughter, be of good comfort; thy faith hath made thee whole. And the woman was made whole from that hour." The bible tells us that by faith we are saved not of ourselves lest any man should boast. And just as we cannot be saved without Jesus, we cannot be made whole without Jesus.

Another process in becoming whole deals with our minds and our emotions. "Therefore if any man *be* in Christ, he is a new creature: old things are passed away; behold, all things are become new" (2 Corinthians 5:17). This process could take some time, depending on how many lies - referring to the lies we discussed in the previous chapter - hold us captive. For example, the definition of a "successful man" is taught subliminally through our environment and media instead of being taught from the word of God. Don't tell anyone I told you this but many men struggle with their identity for many reasons. We are bombarded with images and subliminal messages of a 'successful man' being one who constantly conquers many women and one who has financial success. But what about character? What about integrity? What about Matthew 6:33, which states, "seek ye first the kingdom of God, and his righteousness, and all these things shall be added unto you." Hmmm… I guess it would be safe to say that we need to revisit what defines a 'successful man'.

I often wonder what this world would be like if men pursued God as they do money. I often wonder what this world would be like if men had the same hunger and thirst for God as they do women. I can guarantee you this, the world would certainly be in a much better state than it is right now. Unfortunately, we have bought into the doctrine of the world instead of the doctrine of Christ. Statistics show that the divorce rate in America has jumped as high as 40%. This tells us that man's definition of success has led us down a path of destruction. It has not only destroyed our families, but our relationships with our wives as well. Man's definition of success has derogatively influenced both our sons and daughters; and with our focus on the superficial, it is clear that we have not taken the time to tell our sons that honoring God is important. Fortunately, as a young man I had the influence of a Godly mother who was instrumental in my coming to know the Lord. In spite of this, I found myself still secretly searching to find the answer to the question, "what defines a man?" I remember being a big fan of Elvis Presley and wanting to grow up to be just like him. He would sing the song *"Love Me Tender"*, and the girls would melt. He was the one who would get all the girls and it appeared to me that they really wanted to *love him tenderly*. I said to myself, I guess this is what it means to be a man. I also remember the movie Shaft. I never saw a movie where a guy would always have at least two women under his arms at all times. They would sing the song, "*You know that cat Shaft is a bad mother…. shut your mouth… I'm just talking about Shaft*". Then too I said to myself, I guess this is what it means to be a man. Then there was James Bond - need I say more? Even during my high school years, many of the guys would talk in the locker room about all of their conquests. The talks sounded exciting to my flesh and conflicted with what I had been taught through God's word all of my life. I must admit, the guys made it sound as if I was missing out on something but I knew it was wrong. My concern was always about breaking God's heart. I knew he loved me, and the last thing I wanted to do was break my covenant with him. What God thought of me was of the utmost importance.

In retrospect, I believe my struggle was twofold. First of all, I did not have a Godly example of a man in the home to model myself after; and secondly, the church rarely if ever talked about sex. I only later learned that under the confines of marriage, sexual intimacy is a wonderful design from God. It appeared to me that girls were drawn to 'bad boys' not good guys or nice guys, but something was fundamentally wrong with that picture. I had to ask myself why a girl would be drawn to a guy who would treat her poorly, instead of a guy who would treat her with respect. I later came to understand that the girls were dealing with the same issues the guys were dealing with - needing wholeness through Christ Jesus. And can I just throw in here that there are many names that are associated with men who do not try to exploit women or who do not use women for their own pleasure. The terminologies are horrible so please forgive me for writing them. They are sometimes referred to as *men of God, men after God's heart* or simply *gentlemen*.

The impact that my father's absence could have had on my life was diffused by the love and guidance I received from my Lord and Savior, Jesus Christ. However, the impact that my father's absence had on my two sisters was quite the opposite and quite disturbing to me. Only as I grew up did I begin to understand that my sisters were looking for love, validation, affirmation and security. Our father's absence left a void in their hearts and opened up the door to insecurity, emotional instability, and low self esteem. They didn't see themselves as being valued. Our mother tried her best to provide all of the love and nurturing a mother could provide, but my sisters were longing for the love and security that only a father could give. Until I witnessed it first hand, I never realized the pain a father could cause by walking away from his children. One of the things I learned while my sisters were looking for validation from our father was that it set them on a path to seek validation and approval from other men; men who I call predators. This led them to accept just about any lie any man would ever tell them. After all, the one man who was supposed to affirm them and make them feel secure, abandoned them and made them vulnerable.

A few of the lies my sisters would accept from men sounded something like this. *You are special. There is something different about you. I've never met anyone as beautiful as you in my life. When I first saw you, I fell in love. I felt drawn to you. I have been waiting for you my whole life. My heart skipped a beat when I first saw you. I feel pleasure just being in your presence. I can love you in a way that you have never been loved before. I will take care of you for the rest of your life. I don't want anything from you but your friendship. I thought that I was unlucky at love until I met you. I know we're in a bar, but God told me you are my wife. I own a mansion and a yacht just like Elmer Fudd.* I could go on and on, but I'm sure you get the picture. Even if a woman is married, the predator doesn't stop. He will ask a woman if she is married, and her response will be yes, but because he doesn't respect marriage, her status will not faze him. He will then ask if she is happily married, as if this somehow makes it permissible to be unfaithful. And even if she is not, she will reply yes so that he will leave her alone. Yet he doesn't stop there. He will then ask her if she is happily married to the fifth power. One has to ask, where does the absurdity end? And the married woman who falls for the deception doesn't realize that it really doesn't have much to do with her as much as it has to do with the predator being able to say, she chose me over her husband. Remember, this young man had been taught that conquering a woman is just part of his nature. I hate to burst anyone's bubble but, more times than not, it really doesn't have anything to do with the individual woman as much as it has to do with lust and a man trying to feed his ego.

I now have three daughters of my own and because of what I have witnessed growing up, and Christ making the difference in my life, I totally understand who I am to my daughters. I vowed to God that I will never walk away from my daughters. I understand that I give value to their lives just by being present. I understand that they look to me for affirmation. I am reminded of the security they feel when I walk through the door -- their faces light up with joy. They never have to say a word, their hearts speak to me saying *daddy is home.* I constantly remind them of how beautiful and intelligent they are, and I make a conscious effort to let them know how blessed I am to have them as my daughters. One day one of my daughters asked me why I always say these things to them. I began to tell her, "As your father, whether you realize it or not, I am the first man you will fall in love with. Because of this, you are going to one day look for me in another young man and I want to set the example so affirmatively that when the counterfeit comes your way, you will know it immediately. As a matter of fact, no matter what compliments he gives, you won't be moved - you will have heard them all from me first. As your father, I represent God's love for you -- one who is here to love, encourage, and protect you. I have no hidden agenda. I just want what is best for you as your heavenly Father does." My wife and I tell our children that we can love them, support them, and affirm them, but the one thing we cannot do is make them whole. You can only be made whole through Christ Jesus and once you are made whole you are validated. You will not have to seek acceptance or approval from anyone because you will be complete, *lacking nothing.*

Forgiveness

I remember coming to a place in my life where I asked God, "What is life really all about?" I pondered this because of the many things I had seen. Witnessing people constantly and repeatedly hurting each other and not being concerned about the life of another human being. I saw people who looked at others as prey, as if to say, "If I find any weakness in you, I will take you out." These observations led me down a path of becoming cynical and untrusting. I remember saying to the Lord, "If you just keep people away from me, I will be fine." I came to the conclusion that we are all born spiritually challenged, mentally challenged, visually impaired, and in desperate need of a heart transplant. Let me explain.

As a result of Adam and Eve disobeying God, we are all born into sin. The bible says, for all have sinned and come short of the glory of God (Romans 3:23). So before you even have an opportunity to commit a single act of sin, you are already guilty through the sin of Adam and Eve. Each person born into this world will need to come to know the saving power of Christ Jesus and have their minds renewed through God's word. Until then, we will be what I call both *spiritually* and *mentally challenged*. We are blessed to have sight, but the bible says "In whom the God of this world hath blinded the minds of them which believe not, lest the light of the glorious gospel of Christ, who is the image of God, should shine unto them" (2 Corinthians 4:4). This means that until you come into the knowledge of his truth, you will not be able to see correctly. I refer to this as being *visually impaired*. Another way of saying it may be to simply say *your perception is off*. Look at it this way, you can get a prescription from your eye doctor and this may help with your vision, however, it will not correct your perception, which is how your heart sees things. Until we turn to the Lord, the veil that is upon our hearts will not be taken away. Which brings me to my conclusion; there is no way we can get around the *heart transplant* that is desperately needed. The bible calls this removing the stony heart. "And I will give them one heart, and I will put a new spirit within you; and I will take the stony heart out of their flesh, and will give them an heart of flesh: 20 That they may walk in my statutes, and keep mine ordinances, and do them: and they shall be my people, and I will be their God" (Ezekiel 11:19-20). In other words, a new heart of flesh embraces forgiveness allowing you to forgive those who have hurt you. Without the heart transplant, forgiving someone will be quite difficult. We would speak the words "I forgive you", yet in our hearts hold a grudge. A new heart of flesh also enables you to see that forgiveness is not only for the other person, but also for yourself. With the heart transplant you will be able to see life from God's perspective, thus allowing you to forgive those who have offended you. Without forgiveness you become paralyzed and may miss out on other blessings that God has for you.

Peter thought that forgiving someone seven times would be reasonable, as he asked Jesus, "Lord, how oft shall my brother sin against me, and I forgive him? till seven times?"

(Matthew 18: 21) But Jesus responded, "I say not unto thee, Until seven times: but, Until seventy times seven" (Matthew 18:22). If my math serves me correctly that equals four hundred and ninety times. Most of us have a problem forgiving someone just once -- how in the world can we forgive someone four hundred and ninety times? Well, the answer is, we cannot. Not without the heart transplant and allowing Christ Jesus to become Lord and Savior of our lives. My way of phrasing it is to say, *we have to learn how to live this life walking in forgiveness.*

LOVE AND FORGIVENESS

I have heard the word 'love' used many times throughout my life. If you ask fifty people the definition of love, you will probably get fifty different answers. The way we define love is very important because however we define it will be the way in which we give it and the way in which we receive it, healthy or unhealthy. Most people will give the same kind of love they received (as children), whether right or wrong. However, God's love is perfect and this is why we need his love in our lives. A question to ask yourself is, "How could any of us love another person the way God intended for us to love without having a relationship with God himself?" Hmmm... don't you think that would be somewhat difficult? When we attempt to love someone it is with condition; we do not know how to love unconditionally. It reminds me of something I once heard; love is just a word people use to manipulate the hearts of others, but God's love was proven through action. God gave his only son to redeem man -- that does not sound like manipulation to me. When we expect man to love us in the way that only God can, we are setting ourselves up for a huge disappointment. Let me clarify - only God can love you the way in which you need to be loved. He has to become the lover of your soul and no one can ever take the place of his love in your life. When we mistakenly look for that kind of love from a person, we only set ourselves up for heartbreak.

Learning how to love without expectation is essential to having a healthy and loving relationship. When we love someone we often times expect them to love us in the same manner in which we love them. When we give of ourselves, we expect a certain level of gratitude; and if we don't see it displayed we are disappointed and heartbroken. The key is to love people without expecting anything in return. The bible tells us "Owe no man any thing, but to love one another: for he that loveth another hath fulfilled the law" (Romans 13:8). Believe me when I say that your heart will feel much better. Your hope has to be in Christ Jesus for he is the only one that will never disappoint you, never leave you nor forsake you, never let you down. And when he promises something, you better know that it shall come to pass. The only sure love in life comes from God. Often times even our parents may not know how to love us. Parents can only give what they were given, and cannot give what they don't have.

Parents & Forgiveness

Your parent(s) may not have received love from their parents, and you would not have known this because they never shared this with you. You may have become angry or bitter with them because of how your life has turned out. Well, your life is not over! And I don't want you to miss out on an opportunity to start it over. You will need to ask God to help you forgive your parents so that you can move forward in life. Remember, it takes God to help you to forgive, and it will take God to help you to forgive your parents.

As children we expect our parents to be mature and knowledgeable. Yes, they mature physically but there are times when they do not mature emotionally. In these cases they may have gone on to have children of their own, but yet they were still children themselves who never received healing. It is difficult for us to view our parents as being what I call emotionally paralyzed, and we never think for a moment that emotionally they could be the same age we are; or in some cases even younger. That is very difficult to digest but oftentimes is the case. Hopefully, what I am about to tell you will help you see your parents in a different light and have compassion for them and their indiscretions.

Imagine this if you will, a baby girl in heaven having a conversation with God. God says to her, "I want to show you who I have chosen as your parents." The baby girl says to God, "Do you mean those two people?" God replies, "Yes." The baby girl begins to cry, turns to God and asks, "Why do *they* have to be my parents?" God responds, "I have a purpose for their lives." Then the baby girl asks God, "Why can't I just stay here in heaven with you?" And God responds by saying, "I have a purpose for your life as well." The baby girl says, "But God, the woman that is going to be my mother is on drugs and is going to introduce me to drugs, causing me to become an addict. And the man that you have chosen to be my father is going to molest me and rape me. And because of him, I'm going to become very angry and bitter towards people, not being able to ever trust anyone. Then because of my pain, I'm afraid I will forget that you do love me!" And as she lowers her head in disappointment, a tear trickles down her check. She then makes a request, "God, will you please make sure that you keep sending people across my path to remind me that you do love me, because I am sure I am going to forget." The baby girl turns to God and says, "Can I ask one more question?" And God says, "Yes." She begins to ask him why he would send her to those types of parents anyway. And God responds to her by saying, "Just as you want me to remind you of how much I love you, this is my way of reminding them of how much I love them." The baby girl replies, "I wish you would just let me stay here with you God, because after all, you are going to require that I forgive my parents in the end so that I can come back to you anyway."

Although this is just an imaginary conversation, I want you to remember that God loves us all and wishes for none of us to perish. If we could just get our minds around that, it would help to change our focus and we can begin to see life from God's perspective instead of our own limited view. With that being said, know that I am not trivializing or dismissing the pain that may have been inflicted upon you, nor am I asking you to pretend it didn't happen. What I am suggesting is that you go directly to God and ask him to help you to forgive your parents and any other person who has hurt you in your life. I have seen children who are born unto undesirable parents; and the children actually help the parents come to know Christ Jesus. So remember, you were born with a purpose and you are not a mistake or a freak of nature. God has great things in store for you, but not having forgiveness in your heart will hinder you in reaching your destiny. As Jesus told Peter, remember that we all must forgive so that we may also be forgiven.

Part Two

Mystery of Iniquity

Iniquity is not a word that is used in everyday language but is a word that is quite profound in its meaning. Some of us may not want to become familiar with iniquity because a self examination would have to take place. This examination would force us to admit to ourselves that we have struggles - and just so you know, we all have them. Unfortunately, we live in a world where we are taught to masquerade or put on facades in order to make everyone believe all is well in our world. This is where we make our mistake - where we start living a lie just for appearance sake. Many of you may have heard the saying, "Ignorance is bliss". Well, after understanding iniquity, you will never again think that there is anything blissful concerning ignorance.

What then is iniquity? Iniquity is a weakness in a particular area of our nature that is borne in us as a result of the sins of our forefathers. The bible tells us in Exodus

20:5-6 that, "Thou shalt not bow down thyself to them, nor serve them: for I the Lord thy God *am* a jealous God, visiting the iniquity of the fathers upon the children unto the third and fourth *generation* of them that hate me; 6 And showing mercy unto thousands of them that love me, and keep my commandments." The question then is, how do I keep God's commandments? Well, in my thirty plus years of being a Christian, I have come to the realization that this cannot be accomplished without being born again. The bible tells us in Romans 8:3-4, "For what the law could not do, in that it was weak through the flesh, God sending his own son in likeness of sinful flesh, and for sin, condemned sin in the flesh: 4 That the righteousness of the law might be fulfilled in us, who walk not after the flesh, but after the spirit." Therefore it is of the utmost importance that we come to know Christ Jesus and the pardoning of our sins and make him Lord and Savior of our lives. For without him, it is impossible to walk after the spirit. I have come to the conclusion that our reliance has to be in Christ Jesus every second, minute and hour of the day. We cannot live a sin free life unless we have crucified our flesh with Christ. We have to remember what Psalms 51:5 says, "Behold, I was shapen in iniquity; and in sin did my mother conceive me." In other words, we are *shaped* in sin as a result of our forefathers. If there is such a thing as an *urgent emergency*, I'd venture to say that needing Christ immediately upon being born into this world qualifies as one.

When we are born unto our parents we cannot identify with our iniquities because we are blinded by the bias love we have for them. Whatever we are born into influences us and becomes what is normal or natural to us; whether it is our families, our environments or even other people's habits. If our parents have not come to know Jesus and the pardoning of their sins, the child becomes prone to the same weaknesses. The bible teaches us that the son shall not bear the iniquity of the father; neither shall the father bear the iniquity of the son. However, even if the son gives his life to the Lord and does not have to bear the iniquity of the father, one has to ask what then happens with the poor images the son took in for so many years.

I had a friend who was verbally abused by his father. When we became teenagers I actually witnessed it for myself. I could not believe some of the things I would hear, and to add insult to injury, his father verbally abused him in front of others as if there was nothing wrong with this behavior. I remember thinking that his father was probably verbally abused by his father as well. This is madness! Where does the perpetual cycle end? The answer is that it ends as we accept Christ Jesus into our hearts. Accepting Christ Jesus creates in us a clean heart, and renews a right spirit within us (Psalms 51:10). If we fail to do so, the iniquity trait is passed down from generation to generation. As God said, he will show mercy unto thousands of them that love him and keep his commandments; but he would visit the iniquity of the fathers upon the children unto the third and fourth generation of them that hate him (Exodus 20:5-6). By learning about iniquity, I am sure you can look throughout your own family and identify the iniquity trait. Think on this for a moment -- think about your mother's side of the family, your father's side of the family, and where the family has struggled with the same weaknesses. As a matter of fact, if you have not come to know the Lord, you are probably still struggling with these same weaknesses right now.

My friend, who was verbally abused by his father, did become a believer. He married a wonderful wife and had children of his own. But I noticed something that took place in his life. As you may or may not know, we all have an adversary. The adversary will not try to temp you in areas where you are strong. He will usually try to attack you in an area where you are weak. The bible says, "Let no man say when he is tempted, I am tempted of God: for God cannot be tempted with evil, neither tempteth he any man: 14 But every man is tempted, when he is drawn away of his own lust, and enticed" (James 1:13-14). Your adversary is always looking for a crack in your armor and the iniquity is the breeding ground for his attack. Although my friend became a believer, there was something else that took place in his life that I could not understand. He began to treat his wife and children in the same manner in which he was treated as a teenager. He, like me, believed that he would never turn out to be like his father but ended up becoming the very man whom he hated. This is what is referred to as a *strong hold* in a person's life. The bible says, "For we wrestle not against flesh and blood, but against principalities, against powers, against the rulers of the darkness of this world, against spiritual wickedness in high *places*" (Ephesians 6:12). Another way to explain it is to say, there is more (to people) than what meets the eye. You never know what someone could be dealing with behind closed doors or even wrestling with internally. The unresolved issues that lie dormant are like a time bomb ready to explode, and all it would take is one push of a button and the strong hold would emerge.

In my friend's case, even though he became a Christian, he followed suit and responded to his family; not as God would have him to respond but in the manner in which he saw his father respond. That 'poor image of being a man' that was lying dormant in my friend's mind had never been dealt with or corrected. When the trials of life came his way, he played back the only image that was there, the image of abuse. Images are more powerful than we realize. A person who witnesses the images of abuse for eighteen years will oftentimes draw from that image; whether right or wrong. My friend's only hope is to stand strong in God's word and align himself with Christ Jesus. Let me be clear, just because you become a Christian it does not mean your life will automatically and suddenly become peaches and cream. You do not become exempt from the trials of life. You have to continuously ask God to purge away the wrong behavior that may have been comprehended as normal. In addition, being a Christian does not mean that you are supposed to plaster a permanent mannequin smile of perfection on your face like an actor in a Broadway play; that would be unrealistic. As a Christian, you will still have challenging days, however, you will no longer have to face them alone; Christ Jesus will be right there with you. Believe on Christ Jesus and know that he died so that you might be free from the bondage of sin and that you are victorious through him. Not only did he die for you, he died for you to have life more abundantly.

I would just like to share my testimony with you. The iniquity that was prevalent in my family was adultery on my father's side and alcoholism on my mother's side. If it had not been for the Lord who is on my side, I would have been an *adulterous alcoholic*. I was already in a perpetual cycle on a broken path. Christ made the difference in my life and that is why I know first hand that without Christ you have nothing.

There's a saying, "The grass always looks greener on the other side." However, after reading this chapter you should never think that way again. You should begin to look at people differently and come to the conclusion that everyone has something that they are dealing with in their lives. Instead of thinking that someone else's grass looks greener, prayerfully you will only look to Jesus.

Transference of Spirit

I have heard the expression, "We are *all* God's children" used many times. When I hear this expression, it immediately makes me think of how wonderful it would be if it were true. Unfortunately, we are not all God's children. If it were so, I don't believe we would see the wickedness that we see in this world. First of all, to be a child of God you have to have the spirit of God. And to have the sprit of God, you must be born again. If a man is not born again, he cannot see the kingdom of God. Nicodemus, a ruler of the Jews, said unto Jesus, "How can a man be born when he is old? Can he enter the second time into his mother's womb and be born? Jesus answered, and said unto him, "Verily, verily I say unto thee, Except a man be born of water and *of* the Spirit, he cannot enter into the kingdom of God. That which is born of flesh is flesh; and that which is born of the Spirit is spirit" (John 3:3-6). So without being born again or having the new birth, where you are indwelt with the Holy Spirit, it would be incorrect to say that you are a child of God. You must first experience a spiritual birth before God can become your Father. Don't be mistaken - God loves us all, but we are not all God's children.

The bible tells us, "For God so loved the world, that he gave his only begotten Son, that whosoever believeth in him should not perish, but have everlasting life" (John 3:16). If God is your Father then he is who you will spend your time worshipping. Jesus told the woman of Samaria, "But the hour cometh, and now is, when the true worshippers shall worship the Father in spirit and in truth: for the Father seeketh such to worship him. 24 God is a Spirit: and they that worship him must worship *him* in spirit and in truth" (John 4:23-24). I continuously tell the members of my church that there are many things in life that you can emulate and duplicate, but the one thing you cannot manufacture is the Holy Spirit - he produces a certain type of fruit. Jesus said, "Ye shall know them by their fruits. Do men gather grapes of thorns, or figs of thistles? 17 Even so, every good tree bringeth forth good fruit; but a corrupt tree bringeth forth evil fruit. 18 A good tree cannot bring forth evil fruit; neither can a corrupt tree bring forth good fruit. 19 Every tree that bringeth not forth good fruit is hewn down, and cast into the fire. 20 Wherefore by their fruits ye shall know them. 21 Not everyone that saith Lord, Lord, Shall enter into the kingdom of heaven, but he that doeth the will of my Father which is in heaven" (Matthews 7:16-21). If God is your Father you will spend your time seeking *his will* for your life, not your own will. And we as believers come to know *his will* for our lives through his word. "Then said Jesus to those Jews which believed on him, If ye continue in my word, *then* are ye my disciples indeed; 32 And ye shall know the truth, and the truth shall make you free. 33 They answered him. We be Abraham's seed, and were never in bondage to any man: how sayest thou, Ye shall be made free? 37 I know that ye are Abraham's seed; but ye seek to kill me, because my word hath no place in you. 38 I speak that which I have seen with my Father: and ye do that which ye have seen of your father. 39 They answered and said unto him, Abraham is our father. Jesus said unto them. If ye were Abraham's children, ye would do the works of Abraham. 40 But ye seek to kill me, a man that hath told you the truth, which I heard of God: this did not Abraham. 41 Ye do the deeds of your father. Then said they to him, We be not born of fornication; we have one father, even God. 42 Jesus said unto them, If God were your Father, ye would love me: for I proceeded forth and came from God; neither came I of myself, but he sent me. 43 Why do ye not understand my speech? even because ye cannot hear my word. 44 Ye are of *your* father the devil, and the lusts of your father ye will do. He was a murderer from the beginning, and abode not in the truth, because there is no truth in him. When he speaketh a lie, he speaketh of his own: for he is a liar, and the father of it. 45 And because I tell *you* the truth, ye believe me not. 46 Which of you convinceth me of sin? And if I say the truth, why do ye not believe me? 47 He that is of God heareth God's words: ye therefore hear *them* not, because ye are not of God" (John 8:31-33, 37-47).

The transference of spirit parallels iniquity. Where iniquity deals with the passing down of weaknesses to the third and fourth generation of them that hate God as a result of the sins of their forefathers and them not turning from sin to God, transference of spirit can have a similar affect. When those that have spiritual authority over us are in error, there is a trickle down affect that takes place. The bible tells us, "Be not deceived: evil communications corrupt good manners" (1 Corinthians 15:33). We tend to resemble those that we associate ourselves with whether they are our fathers, mothers, friends or Pastors. That is why the company you keep is so important. "He that walketh with wise *men* shall be wise: but a companion of fools shall be destroyed" (Proverbs 13:20).

The spirit of someone who is in authority over you has the power to influence your thoughts, behavior, and mood. Have you ever worked at a job where the boss was very dictatorial? No matter how outgoing you were or how much you enjoyed your work, the atmosphere and environment were negatively influenced. You probably found that everyone was on edge or unfulfilled, productivity was hindered, and morale was low. Now take a situation where a boss is hard working, has excellent leadership abilities, and possesses great interpersonal skills. Employees will feel motivated and inspired by their leadership. Not only will employees enjoy coming to work, but the environment and atmosphere, which would be influenced by the boss's positive demeanor, would be harmonious. The workers would feel valued and as a result be more productive.

The same thing holds true for a Pastor of a church. The members of a church begin to resemble their Pastor's spiritual life. If he is a praying Pastor, the members will be influenced to always pray as well. If the Pastor displays a passion for God, the members will emulate that same passion. The Pastor has a very unique opportunity to either influence the members unto the things of God or manipulate the members through the word of God for their own agenda. This is why it is so important to know your Pastor. It is not enough to attend a church just because you are religious or just because it has been a tradition in your family or even because you have heard great things about its praise and worship. You should go because it is a sound bible teaching church that worships God in spirit and in truth through prayer, praise and the proclamation of the word of God.

I give every member of my church the opportunity to get to know who I am outside of the pulpit. As a Sheppard, I should be able to live transparently before them as I do God. I have taken notice that if I am transparent, the members become transparent as well, which confirms my previous statement; when someone is in spiritual authority over you, they have the power to influence your thoughts, behavior, and mood. I will continue to use the influence God has given me to encourage people to get to know Christ Jesus as Lord and Savior of their lives. This brings me to my next point. Without regeneration and without being born again, we will continue to live our lives under the influence of our biological parent(s).

I recently interviewed a friend who told me that he never had the opportunity to meet his father but was amazed that he turned out to be just like him; having the same struggles, addictions, and life - if you can believe that. It took him years to come to the understanding that he needed a new father; a true and perfect father, which is God. He shared with me that once he gave his life to the Lord the bondage of sin was broken, thus breaking the perpetual cycle. He was indwelt with the Holy Spirit and no longer under the influence of his biological father. He became influenced by the spirit of God. He shared with me that as he consumed himself in God's word, his desire for the addictions dissipated. He did as the word of God says, and he no longer had to bear the iniquity of his biological father. If you feel there is no hope, you are wrong. There is always hope through Christ Jesus our Lord. Whether you had a good start in life or a bad start in life, once you get a hold of Jesus, your life will never be the same.

Family Secrets

When I was a teenage kid, I remember standing on my front porch and counting the houses on our street. If my memory serves me correctly, I counted about thirty houses. Out of the thirty, less than half comprised of two parents. I always wondered what was actually going on behind those closed doors. I remember thinking to myself, you can see someone everyday and never really know what they are dealing with. In telling this story, I purposely use the word *house* instead of *home*. I would like to point out that there is a clear distinction between the two. A house, according to Webster's dictionary, is *a building intended for human habitation*. Wow! That sounds very warm, reassuring and uplifting. Of course I am being facetious and simply trying to drive home a point (*no pun intended*). A home on the other hand, should reflect a sanctuary - a place where the presence of God is evident and love, peace and joy are abundant. A place where mistakes can be made and you are lovingly corrected. An environment where love is prominent and you are accepted. A home is the launching pad for your life - everyone inside is your support system for the outside. This is what a home should represent, but unfortunately there are times it is reminiscent of a mortuary; where it echoes voices throughout like the howling whistle of a whirling tornado waiting to be filled with sound. I had a friend whose house bore this resemblance. They had cold ceramic floors and as you walked through, it was very still and lifeless. The house was at the end of the street with a sign that read, 'Dead End', go figure! The sign and the inside of the house were like identical twins, forever destined to validate one another and not be complete unless the other was nearby. Ironically, my friend's house was the last house on the left; destined to exist at the end of the street with its only comfort from a sign that read, 'Dead End'! I don't think I have to tell you how much my friend struggled in his life having grown up in this type of dysfunctional environment, where there was no life or no love. He surely became a product of his environment.

This is just one example of a family secret - here's another. I once knew of a teenage boy who for years was forced to have sex with his mother. It was so bad for him that he had to seek counseling when he became an adult. He was being tortured by his mother's behavior and no one knew it was happening. The power that parents have over their children is amazing. If a parent is abusive, the child is torn between the love they have for the parent and the anger they feel from being abused. This is actually too much for their minds to handle. On one hand the child loves their parent, but on the other hand may hate their parent. The loyalty and allegiance that a child has for his or her parent gives a parent so much power over the child. If a child could love a parent in spite of a parent's abuse, think of the love a child would have without this abuse.

I can recall another friend of mine mentioning to me that after his mother and father divorced, his mother verbally abused him for years. When he became an adult and kept having failed relationships, he thought that this could have been the result of his mother's abuse. He then went to his mother and asked her why she degraded him and verbally abused him after his dad left. His mother's response was staggering. She actually told her son, "Every time I looked at you, I saw your father. And because I wasn't able to take my anger out on him, I took it out on you." The mother asked for the son's forgiveness, and the son complied. Anytime the mother had difficulty in her life, she would call my friend, her son, and he ran to her aid in spite of the abuse. Even though she degraded him for years, he felt obligated to be there for her because in his eyes she was still his mother. Although he never felt that his mother loved him, he continued to run to her aid hoping that she would one day appreciate him and show him the love he longed for. What a web to be caught in. The titles 'mother' and 'father' have such significance and influence that even without knowing how to be a parent, a child will still love their parent. That's the power parents have over their children. She had the title, which carried much weight, but had not lived up to its true meaning.

Family secrets can be the death of you. We all have things in our family that do not make us proud, and if you don't expose them, those secrets will be the bondage that holds you captive. When I think about a family secret, I think of something that could make you feel ashamed or a lie that needs the light of truth to shine upon it. I'm reminded of a young girl about sixteen years old that I counseled. She began to share all of her family secrets with me, including the fact that her new best friends had become *misery* and *agony*. She talked about them as if they were real! I told her she was going to have to find new best friends, but she became accustomed to *misery* and *agony* and felt that they were her comfort. She went so far as to say, she would be lost without them. She wanted to keep them because in her mind they were dependable and predictable, unlike her parents. As I continued to counsel and minister to her, her family secret became exposed. Through prayer and humility she began to accept the word of God, and eventually forgave her parents. She was then able to let go of those "best friends" that held her captive, and this in turn allowed her to be freed from bondage.

God wants us to be free from the bondage of sin and he wants us to be free from the secrets which hold us captive. But we have to do what James said in God's word. He tells us to submit ourselves to God. Resist the devil and he will flee, Draw nigh to God, and he will draw nigh to you (James 4:7-8). If we can learn to resist the devil, expose the devil, and flee from the devil, how can he hold us captive? He cannot if we draw near to God. We can't continue to hide from God and expect to overcome the family secrets that hold us captive. If you continue to hide from God, all that you are doing is hurting yourself and your children. Remember, just because we live in houses made of brick, aluminum, or wood it doesn't mean that God can't see on the inside of our homes. Just to give you a heads up, God is not in heaven saying to himself, "Man! I'll be glad when they come outside of that house so I can see them. That new material they're using to make houses these days has made it difficult for me to even see inside." God is present everywhere and is all knowing - God is omnipresent and omniscient. It doesn't make sense to try to run from God. Some of you have been running for so long that you might as well become Olympic runners and run the 2000 meter dash. Aren't you tired by now? All you have to do is turn to God. No one is going to have the answers that you are in search of but God. Jesus died for you almost 2000 years ago yet you have not acknowledgement his sacrifice. Why don't you become the person in your family that breaks the perpetual cycle of the secrets that have held your family captive? God is here to help you. He has said, "If my people, which are called by my name, shall humble themselves, and pray, and seek my face, and turn from their wicked ways; then will I hear from heaven, and will forgive their sin, and heal their land" (2 Chronicles 7:14).

If I have failed to clearly explain how devastating family secrets can be, let me communicate it differently. If there was a camera inside of your house which allowed the world to see your behavior behind closed doors, would you still behave in the same manner? If you answer no, then you may want to look into getting some help. The only place you can look is to Christ Jesus. He is the only one who can heal the pain of your past and free you from any secret sin that presently holds you captive.

Family Secrets and Family Titles

Before a child understands that they are to honor their 'mother' and 'father' as the word of God tells us, they have an innate preconceived expectation because of the titles. There is a dependency on the people who wear the titles, which creates a potential for devastation. Ponder this for a moment. Think of the word mother - what will usually come to mind is one who is nurturing, caring, loving, and supportive. Now, think of the word father - what usually comes to mind is one who is strong, protective and a provider. The potential for devastation comes into play when the unforeseen, unfathomable or unimaginable occurs. We don't commonly associate the word devastation with titles of honor, but often times there is an association. What usually follows the word devastation from a young adult is the phrase, "I can't believe my mother did this to me" or "I can't believe my father abused me". What they are actually saying is that they are devastated more because of the titles of honor and the preconceived expectation of the people wearing them. It is amazing that human beings graduate to titles of honor just by having children, even if they are ill-equipped to wear the titles. I humbly submit that if we can remove all titles, whereby we place honor by remembering that mothers, fathers and even Pastors are human beings first, the impact they could have would no longer be devastation, only disappointment. There's no harm in expecting a certain behavior from a parent or anyone who wears a title, however, forgetting that they are human beings first is what can cause the devastation.

Relationships

You will have many different types of relationships throughout your life which will bear many different titles. You may have friends, associates, business partners, co-workers, bosses, etc. Then there may be your husband, wife, mother, father, brothers, sisters, cousins, aunts, uncles, grandparents, and hopefully your Pastor. But the most important relationship you will ever have will be your relationship with Christ Jesus. As you may or may not know, all relationships require time and effort or they will die. Now I don't know about you, but I find it difficult to give quality time to each one of the aforementioned relationships without one of them suffering. So, what does one do? Given the fact that we only have 24 hours in a day, the first thing we must learn to do is prioritize. We then must learn to manage our time, keeping in mind that everyone will not receive the same amount of time from us -- it is simply not possible. As a Pastor, quite a few people cross my path, including the members of my church. I have learned that the best way to manage my time with my members is to make sure that their focus is not about their relationships with me, but about their relationships with Jesus Christ.

This not only helps me to better manage my time, but in turn helps bring overall balance to their lives. They may begin to notice that their friends welcome them with open arms because they are like a breath of fresh air to be around. Let's face it, if you have a friend and all they do is complain, complain, complain, how long do you think it will take before you begin to pull back from the relationship? Probably not that long!

Another observation I've made is how we as people deal with disputes or disagreements in relationships. We often times go on assumptions or act as if we are afraid to speak about resolving conflicts. Sometimes we act as if bringing them up is taboo to the relationship; however, this could not be further from the truth. Disputes and disagreements must be looked at in a positive light - they are a means of understanding another person's point of view. I'm not suggesting that this is always going to be the patented resolve; however, I guarantee that if the word of God is not the final authority when there is a dispute, you are going to be in for a long night. "Every way of a man *is* right in his own eyes: but the Lord pondereth the heart" (Proverbs 21:2). Need I say more?

Now that we have come to the understanding that the word of God must be the final authority in resolving disputes, let us take a look at another aspect of relationships - *bearing burdens.* Some people think that because you are in a relationship with them, this gives them the right to dump on you. Even though the word of God tells us that we are to bear one another's burden, it does not entitle us to dump our burdens on one another. "For every man shall bear his own burden" (Galatians 6:5). Once we've come to terms with bearing our own burdens, God gives us the blue print through his word, which tells us that we do not have to carry our burdens alone, "Cast thy burden upon the Lord, and he shall sustain thee: he shall never suffer the righteous to be moved" (Psalms 55:22).

It is very important to be selective about the type of people you let into our life. It has been said that people come into our lives for a reason, a season or a lifetime. One of the worse things that could happen to any of us is to have a 'season' continue in our lives for a 'lifetime'. If you fail to recognize someone's purpose in your life and continue to move forward blindly with the relationship, you are opening yourself up for unnecessary pain and turmoil. There will be no way of getting around the negative impact that this type of situation will have on you. This is why we must, and I emphasize, *must* go to God before we allow people into our lives, "The heart is deceitful above all *things* and desperately wicked: who can know it?" (Jeremiah 17:9). In other words, you cannot read what is in a person's heart upon first meeting them. You must go to God, as He knows the heart of all man. You may be in a relationship with someone who God has released from you, but because of pride, shame, or maybe even concern of what others may say, you have allowed them to remain in your life.

I had a friend whose husband committed adultery over and over again, and yet she stayed in the marriage. I would not encourage her to pursue a divorce, as I am not an advocate of such. I prayed that God would open up her eyes, and that his will would be done. My other concern after speaking with her pertained to her mindset while dealing with his unfaithfulness. She would always speak of how much God hates divorce as if he would never forgive her if she decided to leave due to the affairs. Although God hates divorce, he has given us a way out through his word. Jesus said that whosoever put away his wife, *except it be for fornication*, commits adultery (Matthews 19:9). However, my friend decided to use the marriage as a crutch because of a much deeper issue with which she was dealing. God hating divorce was not her real issue. Her real issue was facing the secret she had locked away many years ago prior to her marriage; which was her suffering from low self-esteem. She never thought she was beautiful or that any man would ever desire her; and with the affairs taking place within her marriage, she would now be forced to face these very issues again. She never realized that she was and still is beautiful in the sight of God.

Unfortunately, many people stay in abusive marriages and end up being held captive by their own fears. Not only was my friend dealing with low self esteem from her past and thinking that her marriage was going to be the safe haven, but her underlying issue was her fear of being alone; which is why she married in the first place. It is important to find wholeness prior to marriage so that we do not marry for the wrong reasons. We would only end up subjecting ourselves to a perpetual cycle, suffering emotionally, mentally, spiritually and physically.

I also knew of a man who had problems being faithful to his wife. After committing adultery his wife became outraged. They both agreed that they would seek counseling together, but in the meantime separate for a while. They vowed that should his behavior change, they would reconcile; if for nothing else, for the sake of the children. The wife decided she would work on herself, but the husband viewed the separation as an opportunity to continue being unfaithful. After all, he could then in his own mind justify his behavior. After several months they decided to reconcile their marriage. This would have been great news…*I suppose*, but with his adulterous behaviors continuing the unfathomable occurred. While they were separated he contracted the Aids virus. Whether he knew or not is still a mystery, but the wife also became infected and they both passed away. This was one of the saddest true stories I had ever heard.

I also knew of a woman who had several extramarital affairs. Unlike her husband, commitment and stability of a marital relationship made her feel bound by normality as opposed to feeling free. Having grown up in an environment where fornication was common place she was under the impression that giving her self freely meant freedom. In other words, she identified freedom as bondage and bondage as freedom. Thessalonians 4:2-3 states, "2 For ye know that commandments we gave you by the Lord Jesus. 3 For this is the will of God, *even* your sanctification, that ye should abstain from fornication." Once a person decides to marry after having multiple partners, the marriage itself may very well feel like prison instead of what God intended, which would be a place of freedom. Here again is the challenge - how do you recognize true freedom when for so long bondage has been identified as freedom? This situation made me look at relationships from a different perspective. I began searching for answers from a scientific standpoint, concerning the drive we have for the seemingly unquenchable thirsts for variety and newness in relationships. My findings were quite astonishing.

First, let me go on record saying that I believe in God's word with all of my heart, and I believe that his word is truth. The bible tells us that "Marriage is Honourable in all, and the bed undefiled; but whoremongers and adulterers God will judge" (Hebrews 13:4). So, what would make us disobey God's word and seek after the thrills of variety and newness? My answer is 'sin'. This may not be a popular view, but if sin didn't feel good, why would there be a need to sin? It would be difficult to tempt someone or entice someone with sin if it were not pleasurable. We are reminded in God's word that sin is pleasurable for a season, and only for a season. As I researched this from a scientific standpoint I found that there is something that takes place in our brains as it relates to variety, newness and falling in love or falling in lust. I came across the word phenethylamine, commonly referred to as PEA. PEA is an alkaloid and monoamine. In the human brain it is believed to function as a neurotransmitter, rapidly sending information between nerve cells and altering our mood to give us a feeling of euphoria. For example, when you first meet someone whom you are attracted to, endorphins kick in by triggering special cells in the middle of the brain which in turn produce dopamine and PEA. When this takes place you may notice that you become very nervous. You'll feel as though you have butterflies in your stomach or that you are unable to catch your breath. What is actually happening is your neurotransmitter is sending a message to your brain and you are reacting to the increased level of PEA; which causes you to become excited. There are several central nervous system chemicals called amines which impact or alter our moods and behavior. Some include serotonin, nor epinephrine, epinephrine, dopamine and phenyl ethylamine. I could go on and on scientifically but in short, just as a drug user tries over and over again to reach that initial high they experienced their first time, the same holds true for the person who seeks the thrill of variety and newness in relationships. For those who believe that they have fallen in love, the increased levels of PEA normalize after about 2 to 4 years. For those who fall in lust, the normalization period is shorter.

God has made provisions for us through marriage. He tells us that marriage is honorable in all, he tells us the marriage bed is undefiled; which simply means we are able to enjoy intimacy as long as it aligns with the word of God. However, for the sinner, none of these provisions seem good enough. After researching relationships from a scientific standpoint as it relates to the thrill of variety and newness, I conclude that the problem is not with the increased level of PEA in the brain as much as it is an issue of the heart toward God. None of us can *keep* ourselves; it is done through the power of God. "Now unto him that is able to keep you from falling, and present *you* faultless before the presence of his glory with exceeding joy, 25 To the only wise God our Saviour, be glory and majesty, dominion and power, both now and ever. A-men" (Jude 1:24-25). Remember, "Not by might, nor by power, but by my spirit, saith the Lord of host" (Zechariah 4-6).

Marriage

What comes to mind when I think of the word marriage is, hmmm…. wait a minute, let me collect my thoughts. It is somewhat of a loaded word that many people see differently. Marriage is a lifelong union between one man and one woman. Actually, it's as simple as that! It was instituted by God and he requires that we love and honor one another. He also requires that we give of ourselves unselfishly and be faithful to one another. The love between a husband and wife should also be a reflection of the love of Christ for his bride, the church. "Therefore, as the church is subject unto Christ, so *let* the wives *be* to their own husbands in every thing. 25 Husbands, love your wives, even as Christ also loved the church, and gave himself for it (Ephesians 5:24-25). "They are no more twain but one flesh. What therefore God hath joined together, let not man put asunder" (Matthew 19:6). I would like to place emphasis on "…what therefore God hath joined together". As a man who is a product of the church, I can remember hearing so many sermons on marriage, marriage, marriage. As young men we were told over and over, that one day we would grow up and have beautiful Christian wives. I also heard the young women being told that they would one day grow up and marry wonderful Christian men, or maybe even a Pastor. As wonderful as it sounded, in hindsight I believe that the emphasis should have been placed more on living in singleness with Christ Jesus. Churches must be very careful with what they convey, because the many sermons I have heard about marriage could have been perceived as marriage being the 'end all to be all' of life, which it is not! Please don't misunderstand what I am saying; marriage is a wonderful institution, but not more important than your relationship with Christ.

Paul chose celibacy in his own personal situation. He understood that every man has his proper gift from God and that few have the gift of self control to refrain from sexual relationships. He made sure that he spoke of this by permission and not of commandment. He also realized that if you are not married, you would have a greater opportunity to work for Christ because your time would not have to be divided in having to do the things which would be pleasing unto a husband or wife. However, he also goes on to say if they cannot contain, let them marry; for it is better to marry than to burn (1 Corinthians 7:6-9). This is to say, that those who burn with passion, should marry instead of dealing with the struggle of sexual passion. This brings me to my next point. Without any understanding of the definition or purpose, some marry because they are in love with the thought of being married or even the thought of being in love. Some marry because they have been led to believe – as mentioned earlier - that marriage is the 'end all to be all' of life. Some are seeking a marital status to validate themselves with the titles of husband or wife. Then there are those who are seeking security, healing or even regular sexual relations. Others are simply looking to be rescued. I can now see how the story of Cinderella became so popular. This fantasy has been sown into the fabric of our minds as reality and somehow we have bought into it. The story of Cinderella is about a man who comes along and rescues/saves a woman from… see, stop right there! No one can be your Savior except Christ Jesus. Anytime you look to someone other than Jesus to save you, you will only be setting yourself up for a disaster. In an ideal world, it would be great if each of us worked on our own issues and became whole prior to marriage so that there would not be a *need* to marry, just a desire. But more often than not, you are dealing with someone who is trying to find healing within a marriage, and you are actually "meeting" them on your wedding day when everyone is witnessing you vow before God that you will love, comfort, honor, and be faithful to him/her for better or for worse through sickness and in health forsaking all others, until death do you part. Not only do you end up vowing before God and witnesses, but you vow until death do you part to someone whom you've just met. You see… the whole time that you are in the relationship you are with their representative or an imposter. The representative or imposter doesn't disclose everything to you, so you fall in love. Not until after you say, "I do", do you actually meet the real person. Wouldn't it be nice for two people to be totally open and honest with one another, without trying to impress each other with facades and untruths? Just think how much time and heartache it would save. I mean let's face it, when two people marry, they marry because they are in love and feel a sense of trust, supposedly.

Trust is a powerful word and many decisions in life are based on trust. Trust can take a lifetime to build and only a moment to destroy. The bible tells us to know no man after the flesh. If we just go by appearance alone we will be deceived every time. Reason being, many people have not learned how to be honest about whom they are, and others are still in search of themselves. So, when you think of the word trust, what does it mean to you? Webster's dictionary defines it as *a reliance on the integrity, veracity, or reliability of a person or thing*, but here is another way to define trust. If you are in a relationship and have allowed yourself to be vulnerable by sharing something that could essentially destroy you if it ever came to surface, and this person never uses it against you for self gain, this is undoubtedly trust and you truly have a friend.

Another point I would like to make concerning marriage is that many of us are conditioned to be drawn to the wrong person to marry anyway. For example, let's just say your mother and father married and it wasn't exactly a match made in heaven. As a young girl you witnessed your mother and father arguing a bit and you say to yourself, I guess all married people argue sometimes. Then you notice that your dad is hardly ever home, and when he is, it's as if he is not there anyway. Again, you say to yourself, I guess all married people need their space and time away from each other, with men seeming to need more space than women. Now being that you are a child, you have three things working against you or blinding you without you even realizing it. The first is the fact that what you are born into becomes what is normal to you. No matter how wrong it is you will justify it away because to speak ill of it is to speak ill of the very place you call home. The second is, as a little girl the love you have for your father does not allow you to speak against him, so you justify his behavior and defend him out of guilt. Lastly, your father's seed has been sown into your DNA. These three factors can blind a child and make the child justify everything they see, even if what they are seeing is wrong. As a matter of fact, the little girl may grow up and be drawn to the very man that would not be good for her, just like her father was not good for her mother. This is quite a paradox, but this is the very reason why I loathe the enemy. You see… I think we have forgotten how important it is to wait on God concerning marriage. If we marry the wrong person and have children with them, we are impacting the next generation of children to be drawn to someone who might not be suited for them as well. One day a friend of mine and I were discussing marriage and she was under the impression that her and I would do well being married to one another. I had to tell her that I disagreed. She asked me why and I told her that if I couldn't marry your mother, then nine times out of ten I wouldn't be able to marry you. She still didn't understand. So I began to explain to her, "Although I would be at the altar saying "I do" to you, you are just the vessel that houses the teachings of your mother and your environment. So again, if I couldn't marry your mother, I wouldn't be able to marry you." It is my belief that in most cases, girls turn out to be just like their mothers.

We forget that we have already been conditioned to attract a certain type of person based on our background, beliefs and parenting. This is why as believers, it is essential that we do as the bible tells us. 2 Corinthians 6:14 tells us, "Be ye not unequally yoked together with unbelievers: for what fellowship hath righteousness with unrighteousness? and what communion hath light with darkness?". This doesn't mean that you give carte blanche to someone just because they say they are a Christian. If you are considering marriage, you should still go to God and hear from him. Unfortunately, you have to be careful even when someone *says* they are a Christian – more so now a day than ever before. You may be a Christian who truly understands marriage from God's perspective and the commitment that goes along with it - which is simply, once you are married, it is truly for better or for worse. In the other person's case, they may not understand the concept of being truly committed or monogamous. This is where you, as the devout Christian, can lose. A wonderful marital relationship is one where both people can truly be the person God originally intended. They support each other and never take advantage of each others' hearts. They can "let their hair down" and be to each other what they cannot be to any other person. This is why it is imperative that you take your time and consult with the Lord. If you do not, you will be setting yourself up for failure.

Some people try to use marriage to hide from themselves and from the world. However, marriage ultimately makes us confront ourselves and our fears. And if we think that we have hid from ourselves in marriage, our children will one day stare us square in the face and remind us that we didn't hide at all.

PART THREE

Perpetual Cycles on a Broken Path

Have you ever felt as if you were running, only to find that your feet never left the ground? Have you ever had the same dream night after night that made no sense and made you feel as though you were trapped in an episode of the Twilight Zone? Well, I believe that at some point in our lives we all come to the crossroad that I mentioned in Chapter 4 where we have to ask the question, what is life really all about? The reason this question arises is because at some point something happens in your life that makes you come to the realization that you have been operating under the premise of wrong information. Some may refer to it as a turning point, and others may refer to it as an epiphany. We all come to a place where we either disregard the epiphany; continuing down our usual path, or start seeking a new direction. Make no mistake, if you ask someone what life is all about, the one thing I know for sure is that you will receive a plethora of different answers.

From the homeless man on the street, to the single mother who cares for her children, to the CEO of a Fortune 500 company; everyone will have their own interpretation of the burning question that we all ponder, what is life really all about? As I read the book of Ecclesiastes, I concur with the writings of Solomon. "Vanity of vanities, saith the Preacher, vanity of vanities; all *is* vanity. 3 What profit hath a man of all his labour which he taketh under the sun? 4 One generation passeth away, and *another* generation cometh: but the earth abideth forever. 5 The sun also ariseth, and the sun goeth down, and hasteth to his place where he arose. 6 The wind goeth toward the south, and turneth about unto the north; it whireth about continually, and the wind returneth again according to his circuits. 7 All the rivers run into the sea; yet the sea *is* not full; unto the place from whence the rivers come, thither they return again. 8 All things are full of labour; man cannot utter *it*: the eye is not satisfied with seeing, nor the ear filled with hearing. 9 The thing that hath been, it *is that* which shall be; and that which is done *is* that which shall be done: and *there* is no new *thing* under the sun. 10 Is there *any* thing whereof it may be said, See, this *is* new? it hath been already of old time, which was before us" (Ecclesiastes 1:2-10).

Solomon's view was that all is vanity, so he gave his heart to seek and search out by wisdom concerning all things that are done under heaven, and said that he had seen all the works that are done under the sun; and behold all is vanity and vexation of spirit. I like to refer to it as the *God Complex*. Let me explain. The *God Complex* has to do with someone who wants to take the place of God instead of giving the glory and honor to God. They ultimately want the worship that was designed for God to be given to them. Remember when Lucifer was in heaven, in the most paradisal place that any of us could be. He was lifted up with pride and as a result was kicked out of heaven along with a third of the angels. You may be asking yourself, how would one know if they are dealing with the *God Complex*? If you answer yes to any of the following questions, you are definitely suffering from the *God Complex*. If you raise your children without consulting God, feel that you have arrived to a place where no one can teach you anything, always feel a need to lift yourself up, are a Pastor and want your flock to glorify you, believe that you are more special than others, allow yourself to believe that you are God, or feel that you are the authority on the bible these are sure signs that you are suffering from the *God Complex*. When an individual has a need to be placed on a pedestal, be aware. "Pride goeth before destruction, and a haughty spirit before a fall" (Proverbs 16:18).

We were created to have fellowship with God and to worship him. Somehow we have lost our focus and allowed ourselves to loose sight of our first love which is God. What I would like to encourage you to do is go back over your life and question everything you were ever taught and view it from the standpoint of being true or false. Use the word of God as a point of reference. Prayerfully in the areas which were false, allow God's truth to coat the pain and bring healing to you through his word. I am not telling you to become religious, but I am in fact encouraging you to become spiritual - there is a difference. Religion brings bondage while spirituality through Christ Jesus brings freedom. To not miss the point I am trying to convey, understand this; God created you for a purpose and my desire is for you to reconcile your life back to God through Christ Jesus so that you can live according to God's purpose. As a Pastor, my goal is to help those who are lost and to help those who are babes in Christ become mature saints of God. I strongly advocate to the members of my church to be individuals who think for themselves and study the word of God, "…to shew thyself approved unto God, a workman that needeth not to be ashamed, rightly dividing the word of truth" (2 Timothy 2:15). What I have come to understand is that if we do not reconcile our lives back to God through Christ Jesus, we will be on a perpetual cycle headed for a continuous broken path.

The Temporary Fix

There are people who attend church for thirty years or more, and still struggle in the same areas thirty years later. I have asked God, how this could be? I believe some people become sold on Jesus. Let me explain. Some of you may have heard about alcohol being a *temporary fix*, and maybe drugs being a *temporary fix*. Humbly I would have to say that when some people hear about Jesus and the blessings he gives, they sign up for the blessing, which is the *temporary fix*, not for Jesus. Most people come to the Lord through desperation. A person may have been told that if they come to church, God will bless them with all the material things; a new home, a new car and maybe even a new job. Often times we are not seeking the Lord because we realize we are sinners in need of a savior; we are coming for the blessing and only the blessing. Understand that if a person is in pain or has been oppressed and down trodden,

59

they are looking for a temporary fix. If that temporary fix happens to be Jesus, then so be it. But the question then becomes this. When seeking God for merely the blessing, what happens when you don't get what you think you should from God? Do you leave or do you continue being faithful to him? More than likely you have come to the Lord under false pretenses; seeking the hand of God and not seeking the face of God. Truth be told, you weren't signing up for a relationship with Jesus, you were signing up for the *temporary fix.*

Here's how I see it, you may be faithful to church work or you may be faithful to religion or tradition, but none of these can restore you, heal you, or set you free from the bondage of sin. The only thing that can set you free is the *eternal fix*, which is Christ Jesus. So, I encourage you to become faithful to Jesus by studying his word for yourself, not waiting for Sunday to open up your bible, or even waiting for Sunday to pray. The bible says that we can make the word of God of none effect by our traditions; and that people can honor God with their lips, but their hearts can be far away (Matthew 15:6,8). We do not want to be the people who teach the doctrines of men, do we? No, we do not! So let us follow God, not the traditions of man. To the person who follows the tradition of man, I say be careful. Sunday can become a traditional event, void of any sense of transformation that would ignite true emotion as it relates to your relationship with God.

I used to say that being a Pastor has to be one of the most difficult jobs to have. As I saw it, the church was a place I commonly referred to as the place of *last resort* or the place of *aftermaths.* After people have been hurt or abused by their families or by the world, they come to this place of last resorts expecting an instant miracle and not understanding that this would be the beginning of their new journey. It is referred to as a journey because it will take time.

The first step will be for them to know that they are sinners in need of a savior. The second step will be to repent for their sins and accept that Christ gave his life for them. The bible tells us, "That if thou shalt confess with thy mouth the Lord Jesus, and shalt believe in thine heart that God hath raised him from the dead, thou shall be saved. 10 For with the heart man believeth unto righteousness; and with the mouth confession is made unto salvation" (Romans 10:9-11). After which the journey then begins, from being broken to becoming whole, from a distorted mind to a renewed mind, from a broken heart to a mended heart, and from a hopeless state to a hopeful state - on their way to becoming the person that Christ died for them to become.

I encourage you to take the time to let your children know about the love of God. Love them, nurture them, and let them know that living for Christ, the eternal fix, is the only way to live because he is the way, the truth, and the life. If we followed God's instruction, the church would not have to be referred to as the place of *last resort* or the *place of aftermaths*. Our homes would become a place of worship and, as I see it, when we worship together on Sunday it wouldn't be foreign to us. We would leave one place of worship to go to another place of worship - our churches would become an extension of our homes. No longer would worship be an event one day out of a week, it would become a lifestyle where we live our lives in full worship to God.

Salvation / Spirituality

Have you ever asked the questions, why do I need salvation? Do I need to be rescued or saved from something or someone? How is salvation defined? Let us first look at the definition of salvation. Webster's dictionary defines salvation as *the process or state of being saved. A person or thing that delivers you from evil, danger, or ruin.* So, does this mean that it can be any person, even myself? Why didn't someone tell me this? After all this time I could have just read a self help book and saved myself. Well, the reason no one told me this is because it's a bunch of malarkey. None of us can save ourselves! Salvation is synonymous with Jesus Christ; you can't have one without the other.

Christ fulfilled his purpose by giving his life for mankind. But the question one should ask is, from what did he really save us? Christ saved us from the bondage of sin, the traditions of men, legalism, institutionalism, and 'selfism'.

He saved our souls from the depths of despair. When I consider where I could have ended up if it had not been for the Lord who is always on my side, the only word that comes to my mind is 'ruined'. We do not have an inkling of an idea what is best for us - we only think we know. I would venture to say that Christ has even saved us from ourselves. The bible tells us, "For by grace are ye saved through faith; and that not of yourselves: it is a gift of God. 9 Not of works, lest any man should boast" (Ephesians 2:8-9). If we could save ourselves there would be no need for Christ. But we need Christ more than we seem to know or understand. By Christ giving his life for us he has given us power to defeat the enemy. By Christ redeeming us from sin, we were given a second chance at life. Adam and Eve had blown it for us so we were doomed. Let us not allow time to diminish what Christ did for us on the cross. Every morning that we awaken it should remind us that we are blessed and that we have been given new mercies through Christ Jesus. I have to thank God for Jesus everyday because when I look at our human condition, that is to say that most of us have some aversion to pain, I am thankful that Christ was obedient to the Father and went through the pain and anguish of the cross in place of us. Once we have tasted the good word of God and the powers of the world to come, the bible says if we fall away to renew ourselves unto repentance it would be as if we are crucifying Christ afresh – entangling ourselves over and over again in the very bondage that we were freed from through Christ. "Stand fast therefore in the liberty wherewith Christ hath made us free, and be not entangled again with the yoke of bondage" (Galatians 5:1).

Sometimes it appears to me that we look for something tangible to hold on to as if holding on to Christ is not enough. I like to refer to it as seeking after the tangible God verses the intangible God. The intangible God takes faith to believe in; the tangible God is humans' attempt to manufacture something to hold on to. I guess for some it is easier to believe in the tangible, than to believe in the intangible.

I would like to remind you that the word of God tells us that "faith is the substance of things hoped for, the evidence of things not seen" (Hebrews 11:1). If we are manufacturing faith through something that is tangible, that is not having faith at all. Remember, blessed is he that believes without seeing. As believers "…we walk by faith and not by sight" (2 Corinthians 5:7). When I think of the word salvation I think of freedom. When Christ died, he set us free from the bondage of sin. Don't you want to be free from everything that holds you captive? That freedom will only come as we accept Christ Jesus as Lord and Savior and begin to desire him and him only. Don't forget that where the spirit of the Lord is, there is liberty!

PART FOUR

Deliverance

What is deliverance all about and why is it necessary? The word of God tells us that the truth shall make us free. I remember studying the Ten Commandments as a young man and thinking that there were so many *thou shalt not(s)*, that thou shalt not remember them all, for sure. But when I began to read with my heart instead of with my eyes, it changed my perspective. I came to the understanding that God's word is for our protection not for our restriction. Even when God spoke of his commandment, "thou shalt have no other Gods before me", this commandment was a means of protecting us from bondage. In other words, idolizing or worshipping other Gods leads to captivity. Unfortunately, because of our human condition, our tendency seems to lean towards excessiveness in everything we do except serving God. If we were excessive in serving God we would be free from captivity and bondage, and there would be no need for deliverance.

Let me ask you a question. What is it that you most desire or that you think about more than anything else? If it is not God then it could end up being an idol in your life as a means of replacing God. You might ask, how does this happen? Well, it happens gradually. A person doesn't just wake up one day and say to themselves they don't want to serve God anymore. Nor do they wake up one day feeling that they do not want to go to church anymore. They may however, begin to feel that reading the bible is a waste of time and that time could be better spent completing other tasks. Nothing could be further from the truth. "It is written, MAN SHALL NOT LIVE BY BREAD ALONE, BUT BY EVERY WORD THAT PROCEEDETH OUT OF THE MOUTH OF GOD" (Matthew 4:4). Many people request *things* from God; not thinking for a moment that they may not be spiritually mature enough to handle these requests. Think of this, if you pray and ask God for riches, will the riches bring you into bondage? If you buy a new home, will you have to work around the clock to pay the mortgage, thereby not being able to spend time with God? If you buy a new car, will you miss Sunday morning service while you use that time to give your car the greatest spit shine ever. Do you realize that whatever you ask of God, he could grant? However, his ultimate concern and question would be, "If I grant you that which you *think* you need, will I still be first in your life?" The word of God let's us know that our treasures are where our hearts are. With that being the case, "Lay not up for yourselves treasures upon earth, where moth and rust doth corrupt, and where thieves break through and steal: 20 But lay up for yourselves treasures in heaven, where neither moth nor rust doth corrupt, and where thieves do not break through nor steal: 21 For where your treasure is, there will your heart be also" (Matthew 6:19-21). We must always remind ourselves as believers that if we seek ye first the kingdom of God and his righteousness; all these things will be added unto us (Matthew 6:33). When I give myself advice, I remind myself to wear this world loosely and hold onto God with all of my might.

Do you have any idols in your life that are taking the place of God? An example would be your mother, father, career, money, celebrities, sex, or even your pain. "For though we walk in the flesh, we do not war after the flesh: 4 (For the weapons of our warfare *are* not carnal, but mighty through God to the pulling down of strongholds;) 5 Casting down imaginations, and every high thing that exalteth itself against the knowledge of God, and bringing into captivity every thought to the obedience of Christ" (2 Corinthians 10:3-6). When I think of what the world has to offer, I'm reminded to "Love not the world, neither the things *that are* in the world. If any man love the world, the love of the Father is not in him. 16 For all that *is* in the world, the lust of the flesh, and the lust of the eyes, and the pride of life, is not of the Father, but is of the world" (1 John 2:15-16).

The devil would have you believe that if you are not living as the world, you are missing out on life. He knows his days are numbered so he tries to tempt us to sin and rebel against God. By persuading us to sin, he is handing us over to death in an effort to take us to hell along with him. His game plan is to have us become servants of sin. This is why we are not to exalt anything or anyone above God. We were created to worship God, and our need for worship is as natural as needing food and love. So much so, that if we do not focus on worshipping God we will find something or someone else to worship. There is no substitute for God. Only when our worship is focused on God can our desires be fulfilled. Finding deliverance can only be arrived by immersing ourselves in God. We must turn away from sin and we must repent.

There are many things the world will promise, but when God makes a vow, it will always be kept, He promises us eternal life through Christ Jesus (John 3:16). If we accept Christ Jesus as Lord and Savior of our lives, we can "Stand fast therefore in the liberty wherewith Christ hath made us free, and be not entangled again with the yoke of bondage" (Galatians 5:1). Because "…where the Spirit of the Lord *is,* there *is* liberty" (2 Corinthians 3:17). He promises that "No weapon that is formed against thee shall prosper; and every tongue *that* shall rise against thee in judgment thou shalt condemn. This *is* the heritage of the servants of the Lord, and their righteousness *is* of me, saith the Lord" (Isaiah 54:17). Are you are a person in need of healing? He says, "…for I *am* the Lord that healeth thee" (Exodus 15:26). Are you in need of a father? He is a father of the fatherless (Psalms 68:5). He loves you with an everlasting love therefore with loving kindness have he drawn thee (Jeremiah 31:3). God will never leave thee, nor forsake thee (Hebrew 13:5). God let's us know that he will be with us always even until the end of the world (Matthew 28:20). God assures us of his promises, as it is "…impossible for God to lie" (Hebrews 6:18). God cannot lie (Titus 1:2).

If you don't remember anything else from this chapter remember this, you will never hear of anyone needing deliverance from God.

Free Will / Free Choice

Have you ever asked yourself why you make the choices that you make or why you've made the choices that you have already made? It will always be derived from a belief system that you have. How you think is based upon what you believe, and what you believe results in how you live your life. Would it be safe to say that your life is a result of your choices based upon that which you have believed? I would have to say yes, which brings me to Free Will/Free Choice.

The term freewill in and of itself sounds somewhat paradoxical or even complicated. I have been taught several different viewpoints concerning free will/free choice and will attempt to share them with you. Free will/free choice is not as one would think. As a believer your life is no longer your own - you have been purchased by the blood of Christ Jesus. No longer do you live unto self, but unto Christ.

The way in which I like to approach free will/free choice is to acknowledge the power in choice. Out of all of the choices in life that we are given, the most important choice of any person's life is the choice to choose God or choose man. The bible tells us to choose whom we will serve. Matthew 6:24 states, "No man can serve two masters; for either he will hate the one and love the other; or else he will hold to the one, and despise the other. Ye cannot serve God and mammon." If we choose God we are choosing life and freedom through Christ Jesus. However, if we choose to reject God we are actually choosing to hold on to bondage or captivity. In other words, we are given an opportunity to be reconciled to God through Christ Jesus and through this reconciliation we would no longer be bound by sin. This is our free will/free choice to accept Christ or to reject Christ. Jesus said, "…I am the way, the truth, and the life: no man can come unto the Father, but by me" (John 14:6). We must be willing to surrender our lives unto him. I strongly believe, according to scripture, that God initiates contact with us and that it is then up to us to respond to the call by choosing him. When God was giving out assignments, I didn't stand in the line to become a Pastor. I felt a calling in my life, it wasn't in *my* plan for my life. I have tried many other paths and the only true fulfillment that I have is from that which I did not plan for myself – becoming a Pastor. Yes, I could have rejected the call and often times did, but through God's sovereignty I am fulfilling his purpose and not my own.

God has a perfect will for the believer. Within his perfect will there is a path and our free will/free choice lies within the boundaries of this path. Someone might then ask how it can be considered free will/free choice when the choices we are making are placed within God's perfect will by God himself. Aren't we just choosing what God has placed before us? I would have to say yes. Don't misunderstand, you can choose outside of God's perfect will, but as a believer I guarantee you that the pain it will cause will make you run back to where... his perfect will. The word of God in Hebrews 12:6-8 says, "For whom the Lord loveth he chasteneth, and scourgeth every son whom he receiveth. 7 If ye endure chastening, God dealeth with you as with sons; for what son is he whom the father chasteneth not? 8 But if ye be without chastisement, whereof all are partakers, then are ye bastards, and not sons."

When I think of the definition of free will/free choice, I can't seem to get beyond the word free. I thought that free meant no strings attached. For all intents and purposes, the word free means to have liberty of action, not confined or enslaved, not constrained or limited by strict rule. To have liberty of action, which by definition is the meaning of the word free, would mean that there would be no consequence for our choices. But there are consequences for our choices, whether good or bad. The word of God tells us that "whatsoever a man soweth, that shall he also reap. 8 For he that soweth to his flesh shall of the flesh reap corruption; but he that soweth to the spirit shall of the spirit reap life everlasting" (Galatians 6:7-8). I believe that we have been given free will/free choice but within the boundaries of God's perfect will. Making choices outside of the perfect will of God can be hazardous to ones health. I surely don't recommend it.

For the *non-believer* the word robot comes to mind. The non-believer is conditioned and programmed to make certain choices in life. When you consider parents, genetics, background and environment, are non-believers actually making the choices or have the choices been made for them? Fact is, more times than not, they are making the same choices in their lives that were already made by their parents. One could say the non-believer is a person who has not come into the knowledge of God's truth whereby his inward man has not been renewed. The bible says, "if any man *be* in Christ *he is* a new creature: old things are past away; behold, all things are become new" (2 Corinthians 5:17). So, in essence, the non-believer is making choices from an unregenerate standpoint or from his or her conditioning/programming.

What about consequences? Can you have free will/free choice without consequences? Free will/free choice may sound like you can do anything you want to do or choose anything you want to choose without a consequence, however this is not the case. God, through his sovereignty, gave humans power to make moral choices but there is no such thing as *absolute* freedom. The freedom that God has given to us is a limited freedom. Those of us who are believers were purchased by the blood of Jesus, therefore we cannot do anything we want to do, for we no longer live unto ourselves, we live for Christ. Those who are not believers are covered by God's grace until they come into the knowledge of the truth. In both cases, for the believer and the non-believer, there are still consequences for our choices.

The only thing that is free is Salvation; it is a gift from God through Christ Jesus our Lord. He paid the price for our sins so that we wouldn't have to. If you would like to believe that you have *absolute* free will/free choice, just remember that you are never free from the consequences.

Value of Life

I am quite sure you have heard the phrase, "I am living the American Dream." The question is, are you really? And more importantly, what does "living the American Dream" actually mean? Does everyone have the opportunity to experience this dream that is in America or are we disillusioned? In past years when I would hear someone refer to the American Dream, there was always an association of the great job with lots of money, a spouse and children, the white picket fence - and maybe a dog to complete this so called picture of perfection. But if you don't achieve this "American Dream" are you a failure? Many have been led to think so.

The word of God tells us, "seek ye first the kingdom of God, and his righteousness; and all these things shall be added unto you" (Mathew 6:33). However, it appears to me that we seek to add things unto ourselves and then when we get into a jam we call on God. So what it really comes down to is our value system and our priorities. There is no way to talk about our value system without talking about the definition of success. Webster's dictionary defines success as *a favorable course or termination of anything attempt-*

ed; the gaining of position, fame, and wealth. But what if you never gain a position of fame or wealth? Would this mean that you have failed at achieving the American Dream? Would this mean you have failed as a human being? Unfortunately, for so long, money and materialism have been the driving force behind the definition of success. Now there is nothing wrong with having nice things or money, but the problem lies within our value system. I have heard over and over again that the love of money is the root of all evil. However, I later learned that "…money answereth all things" (Ecclesiastes 10:19).

Here is the problem. As we seek after money instead of seeking after God, money has the potential of becoming a God, which in turn, is idol worship. Our hearts are then removed from the one which through his grace has allowed us the blessings in the first place. It is not the money itself that is evil, it is what we will do for it that makes it evil. I don't know about you, but I have always viewed money as being that which exposes what is already in the heart of a person. If a person is caring, they will be more generous in their giving and more benevolent. The same holds true for a person who has issues with gambling. Without money they might be able to hide or conceal their gambling problem because they cannot afford to frequent the casino. However, with money what is in the heart, which in this case is a gambling habit, will be seen on a grander scale.

I have often wondered what would happen to the world if money had nothing to do with the definition of success and if success were based upon or solely defined by one's character. For example, what if character and integrity were the measurements for success? What if the person who pursues God is not only successful in God's eyes, but is deemed successful in man's eyes as well? What if man's reverence for God or man's value for human life held the same weight or same regard as man's value in money. One thing would be for sure; the taking of another human being's life would be unthinkable because there would be an esteemed value placed on life. As it stands, people lose their lives simply because of the wrong value system. Sometimes I have to ask myself how we arrived at this place. I have come to the conclusion that money and materialism are for some people more important than just about anything else; even the life of another human being. Say what you will, but when human beings lose their lives over something that can be replaced, we have become depraved and lost. What we are conveying is that human life has no real value.

This "American Dream" is actually a nightmare, where people lie, cheat, steal and kill to obtain what we call 'success'. After acquiring financial success people become 'separate' and are looked upon as highly regarded individuals. However, the truth is we should all be looked upon as separate individuals regardless of our financial status. Unfortunately, due to our society's value system, this is not the case. This is just another example of how man places money at a higher value than human life itself. Some may not agree, but the recession that we are living in is one of the best things that could have happened to society. The things which we allow to divide us can no longer do so - we all need each other. In the eyes of God, no person is more significant than another. "Then Peter opened *his* mouth and said, Of a truth I perceive that God is no respecter of persons" (Acts 10:34). Yet we seek reputation in an effort to finding significance within ourselves. Consider the possibility for a moment that although this recession took place as a result of greed and deception, we are faced with a unique opportunity to reprioritize and reevaluate that which we deem as important.

If pursuing the American Dream means to devalue human beings, then I guess I will never dream that dream. I have a better dream, and this dream can become a reality for eternity. I pray that we the human race can value each other the way that God values us, and love one another the way that God loves us. No longer would we pursue this American Dream that only provides a temporary perspective. We would develop an eternal perspective - the perspective that God truly wants us to have, one where life, joy, peace, and tranquility are never ending. Now this may sound unrealistic but, make no mistake about it, it is very real. It is a place called Paradise – the place where God shall wipe away all of our tears, "…and there shall be no more death, neither sorrow, nor crying, neither shall there be any more pain: for the former things are passed away" (Revelation 21:4). We can have this eternal reality as we "…confess with thy mouth the Lord Jesus, and shalt believe in thine heart that God hath raised him from the dead, thou shall be saved. 10 For with the heart man believeth unto righteousness; and with the mouth confession is made unto salvation. 11 For the scripture saith, WHOSOEVER BELIEVETH ON HIM SHALL NOT BE ASHAMED. 12 For there is no difference between the Jew and the Greek: for the same Lord over all is rich unto all that call upon him. 13 FOR WHOSOEVER SHALL CALL UPON THE NAME OF THE LORD SHALL BE SAVED" (Romans 10:9-13).

Prayer

With the hustle and bustle of every day life we can find ourselves so busy that we forget to pray or become too tired to pray. I believe that this is one of the most dangerous mistakes we can make as believers. Even those of us with the best intentions can fall short in this area. If we do not develop a healthy prayer life, we are no different than the person who receives seed among the thorns and hear the word but because of the cares of this world and the deceitfulness of riches, choke the word and become unfruitful (Matthew 13:22). But how does one develop a healthy prayer life? The answer is by first understanding the importance of prayer.

Prayer is a form of worship. Through prayer we acknowledge the sovereignty and power of God with thanksgiving. The bible tells us, "Be careful for nothing; but in every thing by prayer and supplication with thanksgiving let your requests be made known unto God" (Philippians 4:6). Through prayer we are actually communicating with God by simply talking directly to him. When we pray it doesn't have to be formal or informal - we talk to God orally and mentally.

Jesus gave us a model for prayer. "After this manner we therefore pray ye: Our Father which art in heaven, Hallowed be thy name. 10 Thy kingdom come. Thy will be done in earth, as *it is* in heaven. 11 Give us this day our daily bread. 12 And forgive us our debts, as we forgive our debtors. 13 And lead us not into temptation, but deliver us from evil: For thine is the kingdom, and the power, and the glory, forever A-men" (Matthew 6:9-13).

Prayer is an opportunity to worship God by honoring his name and accepting his will for our lives. This is also an opportunity to forgive so that we may be forgiven, and to make our request known to the Father. The bible tells us, "Enter his gates with thanksgiving, *and* into his courts with praise: be thankful unto him, and bless his name" (Psalms 100:4). Prayer is also a time of meditation and concentration on God's power and majesty; where we turn our attention away from ourselves and worship him in spirit and in truth - listening to what he speaks to our hearts. What I have come to love is that after I have disciplined myself for daily prayer, I am renewed in spirit and in mind.

If we model ourselves after Jesus, we would pray for God's will to be done in our lives, not our own will. No matter what thoughts you may have concerning yourself or how well you think you know yourself, just remember that God is the creator of the universe. As intelligent as we may think we are, we cannot predict the future, therefore we don't really know what is best for us. This is why when we pray, we are not asking God to conform to our will, we should be of the mindset of conforming to his will. The only time my peace is interrupted in my life is when I try to do things my way. When we learn to depend on God and trust that he knows what is best for us, the burden of trying to do things our way, in our own strength, is lifted.

Find a secret place that is quiet, such as a prayer closet and "...when thou prayest, enter into thy closet, and when thou hast shut thy door, pray to thy Father which is in secret; and thy Father which seeth in secret shall reward thee openly" (Matthew 6:6). "Take heed that ye do not your alms before men, to be seen of them: otherwise ye have no reward of your Father which is in heaven" (Matthew 6:1). When you pray, remember it is a form of worship unto God, not man. And if you want your reward from God, develop a disciplined prayer life in your secret place.

EPILOGUE

I spoke with a friend the other day who I hadn't spoken with for several months. He began to speak with me about his relationship with a young lady, and how they have reached a point where they are sharing their life stories. We've all come to this stage of a relationship; first the meeting then the dating then the courting and then "the stories". Before he continued, I asked him if he begins his *life story* by speaking about negative experiences. As he paused, I answered the question for him, responding yes. He then asked how I knew. I began to explain to him that many people define their existence through pain. The irony is that we can have a life filled with many wonderful years and as soon as we experience something that we deem negative we become consumed with the negative experience instead of focusing on how God kept us for so long.

This is why I give much credit to actor, writer, producer, and director Tyler Perry. He continuously, through his work and inspirational words, conveys a much needed message which is, although our negative experiences help to shape who we are they do not define who we are.

When you come to the point of sharing your *life story* I encourage you to speak first about the wonderful blessings in your life before speaking about the negative experiences. We should not allow our negative experiences to overshadow God's faithfulness.

For Additional Information about
"The Sins of The Father"
Contact
Prominence Ministries
9201 Bryant Farms Rd
Charlotte NC 28277
www.prominenceministries.org
404-429-5758

To order a copy of "The Sins of The Father"
Call 1-866-774-5647
Diverse Marketers LLC
P.O. Box 78952
Charlotte NC 28271

johnwknight3@gmail.com